I0202485

Stumbling Towards the Desire of Grace

Written By:

Mike Hillebrecht

Charis Academy Publishing

Portland, Oregon

www.charisacademy.org

Stumbling Towards the Desire of Grace

© 2015 mike hillebrecht

ALL RIGHTS RESERVED

This work is licensed under a Creative Commons Attribution-ShareAlike 3.0 Unported License.

ISBN-13 978-0692365229

ISBN-10 0692365222

Scripture quotations are from the King James Version unless noted otherwise. Scriptures taken from the MIRROR Copyright 2012 used by permission of the Author

Other Books by mike hillebrecht

Grace for Shame

Chesed – Beyond the Veil of Mercy

A Kingdom Primer

Eternal Life. Yes, Forever!

My Grace to You

The Forbidden Sermons

There's only Grace

Published by

Charis Academy Publishing

Portland, Oregon

www.charisacademy.org

Table of Contents

Stumbling Towards the Desire of Grace

There are plenty of fish in the sea

but there is one that is mine.
Don't even think about touching it.

Editorial warning

When writing this kind of material English–types have a field day with me. How, you may ask. Well, simply put, they get tense; past, present and future.   Let's all agree on one thing: The bible records events from the past; people read it in the present, expecting a better future.   If you're reading a past event, in my world, you're making a past event present in the moment, especially if you've never read it before. So using past tense wording at that instant takes the excitement away from the message being unveiled right in the moment.   The word your reading is living still, right now, today. It did not die, it ascended to a place where you're also seated. So let's just learn to talk plainly to each other without getting hung up on when something happened, is happening, or will happen. Try to live in the arena of knowing the end from the beginning, now.

Next, there may be couple of you who take offense at just how I present this material. You may feel I'm not treating it with the reverence you feel it deserves or that I'm making light or belittling certain aspects of... well...everything! You're in luck. This book is devoted to your deliverance from offense of all kinds.   I'm quite pleased with it myself because I had to overcome a few on my way to writing it out fully. So it is fully tested and a real eye-opener to a realm of grace you may have never considered.

With this said, I trust that as you read this you will be challenged, perplexed, smitten, drawn into, pulled apart from, and amused at what grace can be, will be, and is like across this universe.

Lastly, no book is completed by one person. I want to thank all of those who helped in editing, reviewing, commenting and just offering gasps of surprise. Thanks to Paul, Sharon, Linda, Kari, Mark and Paul for your involvement. It has been greatly appreciated.

Charis, chesed, and shalom to you.

mike

Stumbling Toward the Desire of Grace

Jesus came to this earth to live the vicarious life as us. In his incarnation he was completely God and completely man. In his divine life he is the creator of all things, everything. Even you and I are claimed as a thing. John tells us Jesus came into his creation to tabernacle, or live, with his creation and the creation, his people, did not recognize him. What didn't they recognize? They missed out on Emmanuel, God with us, and overlooked his human frame.

When Jesus came down from heaven to live in a mortal body Paul claims he gave up his riches to inhabit our poverty. The moment he touched earth, his divine attributes were constrained to only what humans were capable of doing. Jesus, the man, displays what a true relationship with the Father is supposed to be like. However, he had to grow up just like we all do. As he does, he grows in favor with mankind around him and with his Father above him.

Since he lived as we do, shouldn't we know how he dealt with the issues of the soul that seem to plague us so greatly? After all, he did create us and it might be beneficial to see how the manufacturer deals with the desire to... Let's look at his last spoken desire as expressed in John.

John 17:24

(24) Father, I will that they also, whom thou hast given me, be with me where I am; that they may behold my glory, which thou hast given me: for thou loved me before

the foundation of the world.

What you may be asking yourself is what does this verse have to do with the desire of grace? Jesus is pretty clear that he wants us to experience this in his opening of, "Father, I will..." That word "will" in some translations is "desire," an intense yearning, one which gets fulfilled. This is the final expression of a desire which Jesus gives before his death making it a rather important one I'd think. The bigger question though, is it your desire?

The bigger picture

We humans are assembled in three parts: spirit, soul and body. This array with the spirit being in first position is the biblical order for our lives. The soul is our mind, will, and emotions. Our body is the container for these two. In an ideal performance of our lives, our will, a term which also means desire, drives our mind, or thoughts, which create the emotions of our daily relations. Each overlaps the other and work in harmony to create a blissful state within us.

3 John 1:2 KJVR

(2) Beloved, I wish above all things that thou may prosper and be in health, even as thy soul prospers.

Most people will hear this passage and flinch because they believe I'm going to talk about prosperity. We have had this verse handed to us by the temple messengers of wealth to such a degree that we miss the relevance it plays in the practical day-to-day operations of living. First off, this is merely an opening salutation to a letter; a form of greeting someone, a talent most of us have lost in this 140-character-digital age. Our equivalent today would be, "Dude, how's it hanging?" or something like that. What John reveals here is how your health and well being is directly attached to your soul and how it operates. Unfortunately, I would say that 90% of all our daily problems begin in our soul for one reason: Desires run amuck.

Desires play havoc with our thoughts and emotions for reasons many do not fully understand. As a desire increases within us there comes a point where it begins to feed our emotions directly, bypassing our mind. Before you know it your emotions overwhelm not only your ability to think correctly but even the desire that instigated them. Dr. Carolyn Leaf has coined the phrase "toxic thoughts" to describe what occurs when emotions and the thoughts they are attached to run wild and generate a whole pharmacy of chemicals in our bodies that attack otherwise healthy organs. All of this stems from a desire that went rogue. But consider the following.

The things that plague our souls, disappointingly, are things which never originated within our self. Now this statement might seem a bit confusing, since a desire is something that……well how do I put this simply? A desire is buried within the nooks and crannies of our soul. However, several years ago scientists made a rather startling discovery in the structure of the human brain.

While running tests on a number of subjects they found what they called "mirror neurons" actively working in the human brain, regardless of the age of the subject. These neurons give us the unique capability to mimic or mirror the actions of others. This is a no-brainer, right? Who hasn't copied the actions of someone else from Elvis Priestley to a mad boss? What made this discovery so startling was how they witnessed these neurons at work as a subject was mirroring the desire while *observing* the actions being conducted by someone else!

From this discovery a whole body of science has devoted itself to the study called *mimesis*. In a nutshell, researchers have proven how we are wonderfully designed to mirror the desires of others. Now don't think this is merely a game of mimicking someone because it goes much deeper than that. It tackles our subconscious mind's ability to motivate us in a number of ways towards an intention, goal or purpose which may never have been ours. What you are about to find out about desires will answer many lingering questions you, and others like you, have been asking for years. The first question being, Why am I this way?

As we step into this study I want to first soothe the nerves of those of you who think I'm mixing science with God's word. As you will see shortly, the bible is full of examples that science is just beginning to understand. I'm simply highlighting familiar passages that demonstrate this topic. Believers and nonbelievers have all been looking for the Rosetta stone of the human condition, and while I'm not claiming this to be it, it does provide a number of answers to how we have developed into where we are presently.

I want to give a few basic definitions to some terms that will pop up as we proceed. The first is the term *desire*: a yearning, hunger or longing to strongly possess or achieve.

Whether it is wrapped up as a new car, a new job, promotion, position of influence, house, computer, phone, a better school, even a mate, desires are basically the stuff of life we meditate upon to feel satisfied.

The next term is *model*: the main person who represents, or possesses, an object of desire. This person is opposite you in that they have what you seek. Consider the manner in which you dress, how you groom your hair, the type of vehicle your drive, and a whole host of other items are representative of the people you admire and model yourself after.

The next term is *mimetic cycle*: the mirroring of desires between two or more individuals. This is what transpires when you get around people and begin...living. Conversations are great opportunities to see this happen as people begin a topic and as they discuss it each person begins to mimic the gestures and postures of the other while the dialogue continues. It is not a conscious act but rather unconscious for everyone involved. This cycle takes on a variety of shapes depending on whom and how many people are in the cycle. We'll look at many examples as we go through this material.

Lastly, the term *rival desire*: a competing desire present in a mimetic cycle. This is the wrench in the whole social experience. It causes all sorts of dysfunctions to happen even in the simplest of matters like ordering coffee. These definitions are basic and will be developed further as we encounter them in the following pages.

You're not yourself

For the past couple of years there have been a series of commercials for Snickers candy bars which have been preaching a truth that most do not realize. The "You're not yourself when you're hungry" marketing campaign typically portrays an individual in the company of friends who must deal with the change in the individual's behavior which is completely out of character due to the hunger he is feeling. All advertisers understand that if they can create a hunger within you for a product they are pitching, you will do something you normally would not do. This message is very biblical whether you believe it or not. Let me show you an example.

> **Genesis 3:6 KJVR**
> *(6) And when the woman saw that the tree was good for food, and that it was pleasant to the eyes, and a tree to be desired to make one wise, she took of the fruit thereof, and did eat, and gave also unto her husband with her; and he did eat.*

This is a very familiar passage which many gloss over in the area of desire. My claim doesn't mean the subject of desire isn't addressed, but how the genesis of the desire is not understood, and thereby, failing to recognize its true nature, this issue still impacts us to this very day.

Let me start with the fact that science says we are designed to mirror. The man and the woman were created in the image and likeness of God; therefore, they were designed to mirror God! Now before you think I've stepped into a dangerous area here, realize that the Apostle Paul exhorts us in Ephesians 5:1 to imitate God like little children. The Greek word for "imitate" in that passage has the same root word as for the term "mimesis."

So let's consider the desire in this passage from Genesis. The woman and her husband are mirroring God's desire, image and likeness. They have been instructed not to eat from the tree in the middle of the garden. Their life is pretty sweet! Suddenly a rival desire comes onto the scene. This desire is not in the image and likeness of God, but it really wants to be. All that has to be done is for this desire to be expressed towards a mirror and then let the mirror do what it does best.

I understand this depiction may seem a bit too simple but if you read the verse prior to this for yourself, you'll see how this is exactly what happened. The snake spoke his desire to be like God cloaked in language which appealed to the woman. This created a false image she would mirror back to the snake and her husband, who, in like fashion, would mirror it back to her. As the commercial claims, "You're not you when you're hungry," and look at what happens to the woman. She sees first how the tree is good for food. Apparently, she is hungry and she is mirroring the rival desire before her. She is not herself!

Now at this point, we could all say to her, "Just say no!" But there is something else at play here that is vital to understand in the nature of mimesis. We not only mirror the desire of others but also the intention behind the desire. The intention never needs to be expressed. Read this again because it's important. The intention never needs to be expressed. We automatically mirror the intention too. Many think that just saying no to a desire puts an end to the matter. But every desire has an intention behind it and it is the intention which is more potent than the desire. The intention must be eliminated in order to stop the desire. If it is not addressed then the desire may not manifest but the intention will lie in wait for an opportunity to be fulfilled through some other desire.

Did the woman and man know this was happening to them? Do you know that it is happening to you? Did you ever consider how the reason you desire a certain mobile phone over another is because the pony express was too slow to get news across the nation? Come on, work it out. The intention was to get news faster. It began as Morse code, advanced to land-line telephones, morphed into walkie-talkies, and finally into cell phones. Now the desire is to be smart on the phone, so it has to connect to the web of worldly wisdom. And you thought an apple was a weird symbol for a phone. Do you finally see what I mean this desire in Genesis is still being expressed today?

When I was growing up, going to the barber shop was a big deal. It was the place where a boy could learn the rites of manhood away from the prying eyes of the lady folk. National Geographic, Sport Illustrated, Aqua Velva and scented talcum powder were the vehicles of moving a young boy into the rarified air of manliness among the social structure of other male models. The one thing that always fascinated me was the mirrors. When I'd sit in the chair, there was this wall in front of me which sported this humongous mirror where I could watch everything going on behind me. But then this was made possible by another mirror that was placed on the wall behind me which showed everything going on in front of me.

To this day I recall the wonder of trying to look into one mirror to see how far I could see into the depth of the reflection from the other mirror. It was always a challenge to try to count the number of objects displayed to see if they added up to the reflection in the opposite mirror. Now I know many of you have experienced a similar event in your life with dual reflections so I want to use this as an example of what will be addressed next regarding mimetic rivalry, or dueling desires.

Just as in the example above, every desire has to have a model to cause a reflection. Let's take Bill and Tom who are best of friends, having been together since grade school. They never imagined that their assurance of friendship is based on the mirroring of each other's desires. Bicycling, hunting tadpoles, football, playing video games and a whole host of other activities became the glue of childhood desires reflected in, and towards, each other. When one wanted to do something, the other also wanted to do it too.

In the crisp morning of an early spring day, Bill notices Sally Mae in her lavender blouse and bright white skirt and something begins to pull at a primal desire building deep within him. Throughout the day the vision of her taunts him, building in ever increasing measures. By the end of his daily classes Bill can think of nothing else as he heads out the door to meet up with Tom. As he descends the last few stairs leading to the courtyard of the school, he inadvertently bumps into Sally Mae, who is standing on the last step with her friends, causing books and papers to sail through the air.

Apologizing profusely for the mishap, Bill scampers about retrieving all the floating materials trying to determine how to dispense them in an orderly fashion. Sally Mae smiles whimsically at Bill's fumblings and assures him that everything is okay. In the moments required to reassemble the papers and books, both of them have conducted their various verbal testing of compatibility and Bill hesitantly inquires into the possibility of meeting later for a burger to the mutual satisfaction of each other.

With renewed vigor and anticipation Bill bids good bye to Sally Mae and runs off to meet Tom who was waiting at the opposite end of the courtyard. Noticing the boldly emblazoned smile on Bill's face, Tom asks what was going on, feeling a bit jubilant himself. "Oh man! Oh man! I just made a date to go out with Sally Mae!" Bill gleefully exclaims as he wraps his arm around Tom's shoulder and spins him around to face the direction of where Sally Mae is standing with her friends. "She is one really good looking girl, don't you think?" he says leaning into his friend's side.

"Yeah, sure, I guess," Tom stumbles out his response looking at her. Deep inside of Tom he begins to feel an urge to get to know her better. The intensity bursting inside surprises him and he tries to push it aside as Bill talks to him about how he had been spending all day thinking of how he would get the nerve to ask Sally Mae out and then how...

Doesn't Bill know this is boring him to tears? Tom wants to find some way to get away from Bill and try to connect with Sally Mae himself!

Rival desires are now in action and neither knows how it happened; only one will get the girl while the other will have to deal with a desire that goes unfulfilled. The dilemma of this situation is Tom may actually get the girl. Bill became the model for Tom's desire, which is reflected back in intensity to Bill. It's that barbershop mirror situation which these two are experiencing. The reflection is not going deeper, but instead becoming more intense between them. As the rivalry from this desire intensifies between these two it could potentially rip their friendship apart creating deep feelings of mistrust, abandonment and jealousy.

Tom may actually never have wanted anything to do with Sally Mae until his model Bill arrived with a desire Tom, through years of practice, reflected right back to Bill, who being already inspired, increases his desire even more in a reflection back at Tom, who repeats the process again, and again, and again, until... well let's see another example to see where this can ultimately lead.

The desire to...

After the fall of man, both Adam and Eve were removed from the garden to fend for themselves in the wild and wooly vastness called "the world." After some time, kids entered the picture, two boys named Cain and Abel. The fourth chapter of Genesis records a number of firsts with the Adam family: the first mention of children, first mention of sin, first mention of offering, the first occurrence of lying, coveting and murder, and lastly, and most importantly, this is the location of the first human victim.

Many reading the bible fail to see how the bulk of it is written from the viewpoint of the victim and not from the outlook of the adversary. Abel, Job, Lot, Joseph, Israel, David, on and on and all the way to Jesus, each represents the persecuted. By recognizing this facet of God's story, and bringing it into how we have told ourselves how humankind has dealt with Him, you begin to recognize just how our desires affect the outcome of a variety of circumstances in which God is the sole comforter. This facet also reveals a side to the nature of grace that often is overlooked which we'll discover as we move along.

For our dialogue here, there could be no better place to study desires than the opening of the forth chapter of Genesis; it is almost a complete study in the nature of desire by itself. We start off with the most basic desire and its result, the birth of a child. This is repeated again with the same result, the birth of another child. Go figure! Cain and Abel represent the first by-products of a desire from a fallen nature. Apparently Adam and Eve find that there is an ability to control this desire and its result because we are told how some time passes enabling the boys to grow up without the mention of other siblings.

Farmer Cain and shepherd Abel represent the classic struggle of civilizations. One is stationary, depending on the whims of the environment to provide the most basic element to make months of hard, back-breaking work pay off. The other is mobile, always discovering new pastures and resting therein before moving on to new vistas foretelling of a better life just around the bend. We do not know how each of these brothers related to their station in life or to their sibling's profession. Did one think less of the other because of the work they did like we all tend do today to certain professions?

We don't really know much about these two boys, or men, in how they grew up, but they seem to have some rivalry issues present in their lives. The question to ask your self is this: Who's the model for the desire and what is the intention of the desire? Is it the older, farmer Cain, who brought his offering from the field and presented it to God? Is it the younger, shepherd Abel, who takes a young lamb and kills it and presents it to God?

Before we leap in here you better get a handle on a word given in this text that many jump to conclusion on. In the passage from Genesis 4:4 it claims how God had regard, or in some translations the word is respect, for Abel's offering but didn't for Cain's offering. Let me ask the obvious – is God a respecter of persons? The text implies this to be the case in its current translation. However the word for "regard" has a few additional definitions in the Hebrew which sheds a little more light on the matter. The word *"sha'ah"* also means: to look at in dismay; cause the gaze to look away; gaze about in anxiety. I know God knows all things but is it possible this "regard" He gave to shepherd Abel's offering was merely a look that lingered in the dismay of what Abel had done?

Now I know Hebrews 11:4 claims this offering Abel gave was a better "sacrifice" and declared him to be seen as righteous. My question is how did he know to make a sacrifice? Come on, everyone who has any bit of Hollywood in them or has read any classical literature knows that the only purpose of a sacrifice is to appease an angry god. There isn't anything in the text to indicate God is waiting in the wings to clobber these guys for some asinine screw up they made. So where did Abel learn this model of worship? Who told him to take an innocent animal as a substitute for a human and slit its throat, bleed it out, skin it, and gut it saving the choicest organs to present for a grand righteous barbeque? I don't know of a single person who doesn't stop in their tracks at the smell of roasting animal flesh over coals and gaze with anticipation of it being ready to gnaw on.

So is it possible Cain is miffed because he didn't think of a barbeque first since this is what caught the attention of God? Consider how God takes him aside while the meat is roasting and tells him, "Dude, what's your problem! This is a party. Yes, every meal has to have balance with produce, but if you're going to act like a spoiled brat, then you're going to have to live with the results of your actions." Okay, so I paraphrased the talk at the woodshed between these two. Here is the gist explained according to Genesis 4:7

Genesis 4:7 KJVR

(7) If you do well, shall you not be accepted? and if you do not well, sin lies at the door. And unto you shall be his desire, and you shall rule over him.

Let me highlight a few words here because they are foundational for this entire discussion. The first is listed as *"well"* and it is the Hebrew word *yâṭab* and means to be glad, pleasing, and joyful. The second word is listed as *"accepted"* is the Hebrew word śe'êth and it means an elevation or cheerfulness. God says to farmer Cain, "If you're joyful and glad, you're cheerful," or put another way, "you're hanging where I'm at."

The final word is listed as *"sin"* and is the Hebrew word cha ṭṭâ'âh. Its root meaning is to be led astray or miss the path. The actual definition of the word is an offense or offender. Yes, it goes further into the *"sin"* thing.

Another point I need to insert here which will play in this discussion later is the Greek term for "sin." Their word has a meaning that describes the action of an archer who shoots an arrow wide of a target. "Missing the mark" is a common expression which describes how Greek culture viewed the "sin" nature of people. It runs parallel with the Hebrew root meaning to miss the path.

With this being said, I want you to focus solely on this term of offense for the treatment of "sin" because it does not carry the baggage the more prevalent usage has. Don't think for a moment that I'm minimizing this word either by doing this. As you will see, if this had been the proper focus of the meaning from the beginning, we might not have had all the issues we've encountered over the ages. At some point we all have to determine if "offense is the sin" or "sin is an offense."

So what is happening in the dialogue is pretty amazing when you bring the proper focus on the words. God says to farmer Cain, "If you're joyful and glad, you're cheerful, and if you can't be joyful and glad there is an offense that is crouching at the entrance of your next step. The offense has set its desire upon you but you can rule over it."

"Offense has set its desire upon you..." is a vital part of understanding the nature of rival desires. As the desire intensifies between two people there comes a point where an offense is waiting to spring its trap upon one or both of the participants. The Greek word for *"offense"* is *skandalon* and it depicts a trap stick used in a snare for capturing small birds and animals. One of the other terms employed by the Greeks for offense is a stumbling block which trips the person on a path. I'll cover this topic a little later.

What happens at the moment of being trapped in an offense is the desire for something will transform into hatred, loathing, jealousy and contempt towards the model. From this point forward it is not the desire which will be the driver in the relationship but the emotions felt from the offense. This escalation of emotions will lead to an ultimate climax which in our example here is the death of shepherd Abel. This is the final conclusion to every rival desire in society - the death of a victim - which came by the way of a snare of offense. The response is also universal at the conclusion: How did we stumble into this? This is nothing I desired!

If you look at the steps that led up to this tragic ending you will see something pretty remarkable. First, farmer Cain desires something from his brother he can't possess and it gets him all hot under the collar. Is it the satisfaction that comes from being "regarded" from God because of his offering? That sounds too much like a little child playing look-at-me-too-daddy rather than a form of worship acceptable to a Father.

God comes to farmer Cain and speaks about what he should pay attention to and then do. The last thing anybody wants to have put in front of them when they are fuming is advice, right or wrong, on what they should do. Emotions rule the hour, not sound judgment. Any advice that is offered is merely a delay in seeing the end of the blind escalation of willful intent to punish the offender. The soul of the person in this condition is whacked out. The desire has lost its ability to navigate because the emotions have overwhelmed all thinking. In order to achieve the end the emotions require, the person will lie, cheat, steal, even murder to see the offender is put in their place.

This is precisely what Cain accomplishes. He goes out to talk to Abel in the field. We have no clue what was said between them but Cain rises up and kills his brother. I can only surmise what was the thought running in Cain's head, "...you kill a lamb and God is soooo impressed! I bust my balls for months trying to keep pests and weeds from taking out my produce so I'll have something to offer, and you, you take a lamb, something you didn't have to do anything with except move it along from one brook to the next, and kill it! Well if you want to see killing work on your behalf, try this on for size..." Believe it or not, farmer Cain is mirroring an amped-up intention from the desire of shepherd Abel that gained him regard with God.

When God comes to Cain and asks him where his brother is, Cain lies. Cain lies to the one who knows all things! When emotions are rampant, the only thing you can think about is how am I going to get this situation back under control. A lie merely is a means to ignore the reality of where you are from where you want to be but can't seem to get there. The hope is that by lying you can deflect a new desire for truth long enough to get your bearings. Regrettably, this never happens since a lie requires another lie to support it which can only be held up by a well-matched desire. It is difficult to model a desire to support a lie and sustain it for any length of time. This is why compulsive lairs go from one lie to the next because they haven't been able to firmly establish a model desire to support any lie they've told. This hinders them from being able to reflect a desire to others who will reflect it back to them thereby strengthening the desire the lie is built on.

I realize at this point how you might think this is a bit far-fetched so let me show you the importance of this matter by jumping ahead to the children of Israel when they receive the ten commandments from God. Moses comes down from the mount with two tablets in his hands only to witness the desires of a million people running amuck. On one tablet, five commandments dealing with how this hormonally challenged group of people were to relate with God. Seeing a golden idol that they're flinging themselves about lets Moses know how his efforts these past forty days have been for nothing. They can't even get the first thing right! Chuck that tablet. It is the other tablet I want to look at anyway.

This is the tablet many have preached about as the commandments that deal with our actions towards others, or our brothers. So let me ask, in my best David Letterman impersonation, what are the commandments on this tablet starting at number ten? I know some of you are scratching your head thinking who starts at ten, why not start at six?

Look if you know anything about raising kids, when you've got a list of things you want them to do, you bracket the list with the most important things at the beginning and at the end. They will always remember the first and last thing you said to them; the rest is mental airtime for their own pity party.

So what is the tenth commandment? Here is a clue: it is the longest commandment. Here it is for you from Exodus 20:17.

> *You shall not covet your neighbor's house, you shall not covet your neighbor's wife, nor his manservant, nor his maidservant, nor his ox, nor his ass, nor any thing that is your neighbor's.*

The last commandment God wants them to remember, and of course follow, is not to covet the things of their neighbor. "Covet" is one of those antiquated words which let people know you're trafficking in the Elizabethan Era, so here is a modern translation for you. "Covet" means to greedily lust and desire for those things you don't have with the intent of gaining them at whatever the cost to yourself, friends, family or associates. Picture Black Friday in Las Vegas and you're almost there.

Clearly God thinks desires are rather important and how we need to control them. If you're still not convinced, look at this arrangement of the commandments. (10) Don't desire the things of your neighbor because it will cause you to (9) bear a false witness against them to obtain it, or (8) steal from them to get it, even (7) commit adultery with their spouse as a means to secure it, or (6) kill to finally gain what you weren't suppose to have in the first place. There they are in order. And Moses decided that the children of Israel wouldn't even understand these so he chucked them too!

Have you ever considered the reason that these five commandments were given to the children of Israel by God was simply because Cain blew it and God did not want the issues of desire to affect how Israel entered into their promise? After all God did warn Cain, but the emotions of the event overrode any chance of wisdom to prevail.   And even when these commandments were first given, emotions were running rampant, granted not like Cain and Abel, but blasting into the stratosphere as the mirrored desires of a million people sought to be fulfilled all at once! How do you think God, who was on the top of the mount with Moses, knew something was going on down in the camp if the flames being released from those desires weren't so blazing hot!

It is at about this time those who are bona fide grace believers should rise up and shout with ferocity, "But I'm not under the law! Christ is the end of the law!" You are correct. But let me show you something not to try to convince you that you're wrong or right, but the importance of this matter independent of the law.

In the story of the rich young ruler there is this curious claim by Jesus towards this up and coming entrepreneur. The start of the story is pretty standard stuff as this young chap runs up to Jesus and kneeling down to him asks Jesus, "Good teacher, how may I inherit eternal life?" When was the last time you asked this question? I know it is something that is on my mind every day at least three, no maybe four times a day. Come on buddy, why are you being so arrogant? "Inherit" means someone has to die and leave you the wealth they have amassed during their life's work. Does the term "trust fund baby" ring any bells? Is this how our kind lad earned his title of rich, YOUNG ruler?

Then consider this "eternal life" theme. Is he so bored with the challenges that everyday life hands out that a.) He needs a fresh challenge which is worthy of his stature or, b.) This is his way to escape the pressures that are too great for him to deal with? I might think it is the latter considering how the text says he ran to kneel at Jesus' feet. There are not many people who ran to Jesus accept those who wanted to be delivered from something.

Now some of you might take exception to this line of questioning because there doesn't seem to be anything in the three gospel accounts of this meeting to suggest this cheeky fellow isn't sincere in his question. That is until Jesus answers him!

"Good...!" Dude, you opened a whole can of worms with that claim. Let's not skirt the issue here and cut right to the chase: Eternal life stood right next to another tree which gave you the "ability" to distinguish good from evil. Why didn't he just call Jesus an evil teacher? It would have meant the same thing as, "I'm helpless in thinking for myself because someone tricked me." Yet, Jesus takes the high road in this matter and exposes this chap with precision. "There is no one good except God." How's that for a good cold slap in the face? As noble as your question may be, your intentions now have to pass muster with the one who created you.

Next, Jesus hits him in the gut with this: "You know the commandments: Don't commit adultery, kill, steal, bear false witness, and honor your father and mother." Does this list look familiar? Yes, that is right; it is the fifth through the ninth commandment. Notice the inclusion of the fifth, to honor your parents, which is rather fitting here if you'll recall how the Apostle Paul says this is the only commandment with a promise. The promise is long life, which not quite eternal, is a worthy life nonetheless.

But notice what commandment is missing? The tenth, the desire commandment. Do you find this a bit curious? I mean Jesus slaps the goodness out of this guy and then forgets to tell him what the reason was for it. Some of you might think I'm nitpicking here, others of you probably are still trying to figure out what I'm talking about, while the rest of you are sitting on the edge of your seat waiting anxiously for the next pearl to descend into to your lap. Before I give that pearl to you, let me back up a slight bit to show you why the fifth commandment is critical here.

If you remember from a page or two back I spoke about the arrangement of the last five commandments and how if you read them backwards they convey the path of destruction that can ultimately happen when you chase after desires. The sixth commandment which is do not kill is the last straw of a desire out of control. However, now watch what happens when you bring in the fifth commandment. Pulling the last straw does not honor your father and mother and when you're caught for your deeds, it will surely shorten your life.

Also, recall how I stated that if you're going to give a list to someone, you position your most important subjects at the beginning and the end. Notice how the fifth commandment of honoring your father and mother is the last one given to this young man. His response is classic, "I have done these from my youth." I believe he glazed over when Jesus began telling him the commandments, not because he had committed any of them, but because he had heard this so many times it didn't have any teeth left in it to make an impression. So when Jesus finishes with honoring your father and mother he snaps back to reality and bites into the image of a young child who always tries to honor his parents. Regrettably, his response is going to get the better of him.

Jesus looked at him and lovingly states he lacks one thing. That "love" thing blows the minds of people. Did he love him because he knew and followed the commandments or because he was deficient in an area of his life and came to find an answer that would make him whole? Or is it possible in this instance we are seeing Jesus model a desire directly from the Father which He wants the young ruler to mirror in return? Before you cast this suggestion aside you better prepare yourself for the shock which is to come to this young man, because Jesus is about to pull out the tenth commandment on him.

"Sell all that you have and give it to the poor and you will have treasure in heaven…" What are you stuck to? What have your desires attached you to that you can't break their hold? Is it things or positions of influence? Are you clamoring to be noticed or does your recognition need to be guarded? It might be possible that the actions of our young man never measured up to who his parents thought he should be and try as he might, he couldn't seem to get them to look favorably upon him. Even this proposed asset liquidation, while applauded by the public, could gain him nothing but ridicule from those he desired to honor. Obviously this is just speculation, since all we know from his response was that he became depressed and left. The writers tell us he owned many possessions which really is a bible code for he was owned by many possessions.

The desire of all nations...

I'm going to step back from what transpired with the Adam family in Genesis 4 so we can move ahead to look at how someone successfully ruled over his desires. I want to pull out the mechanics of this mimetic theory to show you how the Genesis 3 account was properly addressed in the temptation account of Jesus in Matthew 4.

Man was created in the image and likeness of Elohim, who I like to call, the plurality of singularity. Man was designed to mirror the desires of others, in this case, the love of Elohim, from the creation. The man is placed in the garden with the instruction he could eat all things except the fruit from the tree in the center of the garden. Next, the animals are brought before the man so he could see there was nothing in them for the man to reflect. The woman is then brought forth from his side and they begin tending to the domain assigned to them, mirroring the desires of each other and Elohim.

The enemy, whose desire it is to be worshiped like Elohim, comes into the garden and expresses his rival desire to a being designed to mirror desires. Using language that appeals to the appetite of the woman, the enemy conveys the nature of his desire describing how he lacks the wisdom needed to be like God. The present hunger in the woman reflects the nature of this rival desire back to the enemy which she believes to be true, causing her to see the fruit on the tree as desirable for food and wisdom to be like God. She eats it and gives it to the man, who consumes it too. Their eyes are now open to the effects of the truth of a competing desire. From this point forward, mankind has been spiraling through this mimesis process causing strife and contention at every turn.

The term "incarnate" means to go from a higher state to a lower state. It is the descriptor for the Son of God, Jesus, who while God, came into this world in the form of a man, being the expressed image and likeness of the invisible Father. Completely God and completely man. The two identities never mingled as long as he resided on this earth. He was confined to the nature of the environment he was in, just like you and me. The depth of this is something for a later discussion, so let me just say how Jesus, the man, lived mirroring the desires of others just as we do. What is vital in this claim is who was he mirroring?

At the beginning of his ministry, Jesus is baptized and then propelled into the wilderness by the Spirit. After forty days of fasting he is hungry. Here is the keystone moment to see if he will be himself in the depth of hunger. The enemy shows up and expresses a rival desire, the exact same one given to the woman in the garden, veiled to appeal to the appetite of a human. "If you are the Son of God..." reveals a reflection that is recognized and a desire to be like it. It demonstrates a fixation on a singular point of interest. "...Man does not live by bread alone but..." reveals the focus of reflection in the midst of competing desires.

Confounded by the response of Jesus, the enemy takes a different tack to express his desire, one which conveys a truth about the kingdom of God but challenges the purpose of authority. "...they shall bear thee up..." conveys the desire for a position to be sought after from a fallen subject, while "...shall not tempt..." readily acknowledges how a rival desire will not step into the shoes of the true identity which is being reflected in the kingdom.

The enemy now realizes he has to deal with someone who obviously understands the design of their nature. So he pulls out all the stops and blatantly does the one thing that is unexpected from the father of all lies - he tells the truth. "...if you shall fall down and worship me..." is about as raw a desire gets in being conveyed to another. "...be gone..." is the rebuke. All desires recognize this command and obey through dissipation.

In the temptation of Jesus we vicariously live out the original design of mirroring the desires of the Father, affirming the original intent of love. However you may recall how I stated previously that mimesis deals not only with mirroring the desire but it also addresses mirroring the intention of the desire even if the intention is never conveyed. Jesus obviously dealt with the rival desire but what happened to the intention? I submit to you that even here he conquered it, but not how you might think.

The first temptation dealt with calling upon a divine nature for supplying food to satisfy a hunger. In the feeding of the five thousand Jesus, under his human nature, reflected the Divine love to supply to the hungry. The second temptation to be lifted high so angels would protect him was dealt with when humans lifted him high upon a cross for all men to see that the legions of angels of His kingdom were held at bay. The third temptation dealt with the kingdoms of this world in exchange for false worship. Jesus handled this in the Ascension to a throne above all powers, rulers and kingdoms of this world. In each instance the desire was rebuked, however, the intention behind them was fulfilled according to the image Jesus was reflecting from the Father.

How to stumble with grace...

When I was an aspiring boy scout, there was an annual event we eagerly anticipated called "Wood Camp." A fun-filled week away from the family spent in the wonders of the outdoors, devoted to cutting down trees and creating massive amounts of firewood which were sold to fund the other events of the year. It was the best! Living in tents with your friends; eating around a campfire; going to the bathroom in the woods; no bathing for a week! Who would not want to be there at 12 years of age?

One of the rituals that always occurred was the proverbial snipe hunt. For those of you who have never graduated this rite of passage or never heard of such a thing, here are the particulars. A snipe, the neophyte is told, is a nocturnal, flightless bird which is the dumbest bird in the forest, thereby making it so easy to trap. A group of boys, outfitted with branches, spread throughout the forest underbrush yelling "Here snipe," while hitting the foliage with their branches. This is done as a means of herding the snipe towards the trap, a box supported on one end with a notched stick connected to a string that was spread out some twenty feet to a boy hiding behind a bush patiently waiting for the snipe to seek shelter under the box. When the snipe runs under the box, the string would be pulled causing the stick to drop and the box along with it, trapping the snipe inside.

Being the person responsible for the care of the box was a big deal and it was only a position determined after a week's worth of snipe hunt regaling had incited the uninitiated to duke it out for the position. Well, not really fighting - which was never encouraged or condoned - but by trying to perform deeds worthy of the position. The neophytes who were unable to hold the position were packed off to the sidelines for the duration of the hunt so they could stew in their dishonor.

After dinner had been consumed and the camp site had been properly policed for garbage, the troop of herders and the trap box champion would venture into the darkening forest to a predetermined spot where the box would be set up and final instructions would be made for the entire troop. Great was the anticipation for the catch!

In retrospect, it never truly occurs to a young mind how herders leaving from the box yelling "here snipe" and beating the brush, actually encourages the snipe to run away from the box. It also never seems to fit that as the voices get further away, the sudden stillness present in the woods should indicate how you've been left alone. Even the constant strain to see the box through the bush you're hiding behind in a dark environment seems to just be a part of the rich history of the primordial nature of hunting. Sure, it does get cold, and more and more your eyes find it difficult to stay open as the toll of a full day chucking wood begins to buddy up with a high protein and carbohydrate dinner. So you toy with the string, pulling on it to make sure it remains taut, only to hear the thud of the box on the ground, causing you to scramble to reset the stick, hoping the snipe wasn't scared off by the noise as it approached the safety of shelter.

There really is no telling how long it takes for each person to realize the true nature of the hunt. It's not the bird who is to be trapped, it's you. Trapped by a prank, there is also something much deeper. The length of time spent in the darkness realizing there really is no snipe coming your way gives way to how do you face your "friends" whom you have permitted to perform this prank upon you. This period of time is the gestation period for nurturing an offense at them, and the longer you linger the greater its emotional intensity. Some have been known to stay out there all night nursing the offense. When they sheepishly enter the camp at the wee hours of dawn they are a changed man for the experience.

This might appear as a filler story but it has great implications into what you are about to study on the nature of offense and how it operates. Let's go see how Jesus dealt with it.

Matthew 16:21-23 KJVR

(21) From that time forth began Jesus to show unto his disciples, how that he must go unto Jerusalem, and suffer many things of the elders and chief priests and scribes, and be killed, and be raised again the third day.

(22) Then Peter took him, and began to rebuke him, saying, Be it far from you, Lord: this shall not be unto you.

(23) But he turned, and said unto Peter, Get you behind me, Satan: you are an offense unto me: for you regard not the things that be of God, but those that be of men.

Poor Peter. Apparently he didn't read the corporate memo. Just a few verses prior to this passage Peter has declared by revelation that Jesus is the Messiah who all of Israel has been anticipating. Finally, they would be able to once again cast off the yoke of bondage from the Roman scourge who had held them powerless in their own land for far too long. Finally, a king – but not any king – one from the line of David, would rule as the prophets had declared so many lifetimes ago. Finally, Israel would once again be a country on the world theater who would command their own destiny. Finally……snap out of it, dude, you're an "offense!" No not you Peter, the influence behind your desires of global greatness and domination, things that aren't in God's playbook.

The term "offense" is the Greek word *skandalon* from where we get the word scandal. Scandals are the stuff of tabloids; prying eyes catching covers being lifted in matters where eyes shouldn't be looking, right? That is how we see it today, but actually the word represents an object or desire which causes someone to stumble or get caught in a trap resulting in shame and disgrace.

We're told in the temptation account of Jesus how the devil went away waiting for a time that would be more appropriate for him and apparently he is still searching for that moment because Jesus recognized him in a heartbeat. What I want to draw your attention to is how all Peter did was express a rival desire, which was that Jesus shouldn't die, and Jesus caught satan in his ploy to use the desire of a man to deflect the plan of God. Realize Jesus did not claim that Peter was a sinner, he said you're being used, and if I follow you're plan and its path, that is the sin all men have committed.

Now you have got to be aware of the fact of how Peter was just following his heart, but it was a heart which had been shaped by the desires of the people he had grown up with who were the product of a culture shaped by desires from thousands of years. Yes, I know Jesus grew up in the same environment with the same influences, however, Jesus knew whose desires to follow simply by the commitment of the relationship he clung to.

This brings up a vital point to understanding the nature of desires: Cultures have desires that we mirror too. Often we succumb to the pressure of our family, our scout troop, neighborhood, church, political party, city, state and nation to see that a corporate desire is met. This is what Peter is reflecting, the national desire of Israel for a strong reigning Messiah. But Jesus knows this is not on the agenda anytime soon for his Father. So Peter becomes an offense. Even later on when Jesus goes into Jerusalem he will intentionally keep himself away from those who wish to make him a king even if it means them doing it by force. What is interesting at this point is how Paul later comments to the church in Corinth that a crucified messiah is an offense to the Jews and foolishness to Greeks. What Jesus lived and how he lived is the offense which caused an entire nation to stumble.

Is it possible that the cross is the trap stick holding up the box we've put God in and we're waiting behind a bush ready to pull the string so we'll finally capture the lost? Are we offended that our trap doesn't seem to work as we leave the box of our churches proclaiming to the forest of humanity that our god is trying to trap them in his love? Has your church life become a snipe hunt for god?

The last stumble to a desire...

Have you ever considered what manner of offense we are by being in Jesus?

Isaiah 8:14-15 KJVR

*(14) And he shall be for a sanctuary; but for a stone of stumbling and for a rock of offense to both the houses of Israel, for a gin and for a **snare** to the inhabitants of Jerusalem.*

*(15) And many among them shall stumble, and fall, and be broken, and be **snared**, and be taken.*

Matthew 18:5-7 KJVR

(5) And whoso shall receive one such little child in my name receiveth me.

*(6) But whoso shall **offend** one of these little ones which believe in me, it were better for him that a millstone were hanged about his neck, and that he were drowned in the depth of the sea.*

*(7) Woe unto the world because of **offenses**! for it must needs be that **offenses** come; but woe to that man by whom the offense cometh!*

Verse 14 from the passage in Isaiah is the same one Paul uses in Romans 9 to demonstrate how Israel responded to the work and ministry of Jesus. We know that he is the rock, but no one wants to call him the rock of offense! So we devise ways to get around this truth and only end up ensnaring ourselves. The passage from Matthew is where the rock of offense is telling his disciples to get into the kingdom of God you have to be as a child.

You may notice I've highlighted a few words here, primarily "offense" or "offend." This is the same Greek word where we get our word "scandal or scandalous." As I stated earlier its definition is a trap, especially the kind of snare which employs a trip stick used to trap small birds. So according to the Greek writings, Jesus is the rock of scandal, a trap designed to ensnare.

Consider this, every week wherever Jesus is being preached a scandal is developing. In every meeting where grace through Christ is proclaimed, offense and scandal should be expected. Wherever you go and talk about the love of God and the gift of His son you should encounter offense and scandal.

Now most people are too politically correct to seek after offense or scandal, they after all represent the Prince of Peace. The paradox of the kingdom is that scandal and offense are expected when you talk about the Prince of Peace. How can this be possible? Remember how a scandal is a trap or a snare. When you employ it properly you catch your prey, yet when used improperly, the trap often snares you. Don't think it's possible?

How many times have you been offended by a verse or passage out of the bible, even to the point where you refuse to even read it again? How about a difficult passage you don't talk to anyone about because you're not even sure how it really applies to you? How about speaking in tongues or laying on of hands? How about the claim that grace covers all of your sins, past, present and future? How about the blessing of the Lord to enrich your business, family or household? How about any doctrine which is different from what you believe and won't have anything to do with it because it's...get the point? Jesus said offenses come and woe to the man who the offense comes by.

So let me ask you, are you gleefully expecting to be rocked by a scandal when you speak about Jesus next? If not, I might question whether you believe in him as the Rock of Offense and might even be offended he would assume such a place of recognition in your life. The paradox of the rock is that it provides shelter while also causing you to stumble and be crushed by its offense. You gotta love grace more in light of the scandal that is following you!

So many believers are exasperated with their walk. They have a desire to be closer to God yet feel distant for reasons they can't express. Let me make a suggestion. You are mirroring the desires of everyone else more than yours. This is why our soul is so vexed. Our minds are being bombarded by the thoughts of others, our emotions are trying to express or suppress this overload, and our will is battling the onslaught of intentions we never conceived for ourselves. This is all because we are designed to be a mirror. You need to stop and determine what rival desire and intention is being mirrored by you. Then you must remember how you are the temple of God and God's word says the desire of all nations would come to His temple. That desire is Jesus and his Spirit which resides in you. Now you have all the tools you need to imitate God as a child. There is no distance in your reflection of our Father.

I want you to read something which speaks directly to this matter of our desires.

> "This wisdom does not originate from above, but is clearly reduced to a kind that is earthly, ruled by the senses and dictated to by demons. An environment of envy and rivalry is conducive to confusion and disorder and all kinds of worthless pursuits...What is it that triggers disputes and fighting? Is it not selfish desires that people host with them; wars are born when one feels that the other has something that he doesn't have. You allow your heart to become so consumed with longing for something that you don't have until you are ready to kill for it. Then you are still not satisfied. What you want keeps evading you; you quarrel and strive, and you just can't get it. If you are desperately unfulfilled why don't you simply ask God to give you what you need? You have asked, but God seems

reluctant to give it to you, you may say. But when your motivation is to get something just so that you can squander it on yourself, you are doing it all wrong!

Adultery, whether it is the husband or the wife that does the flirting, is destructive. Can't you see that even though the world system might approve of such behavior, it is contrary to God's design for you? Whose friend do you want to be? Are you prepared to distance yourself from God just to win the applause of the world? Scripture is not quoting empty words when it states that God yearns with jealous expectation over the spirit which he has made to inhabit us. His gift of grace surpasses the onslaught of lust. Scripture says God opposes the haughty and gives grace to the humble. Yield yourselves in total abandonment under God's authority so that the devil knows who backs you when you resist him, he will scramble away from you."

This passage from the Mirror translation of the book of James 3:15-16 and 4:1-7 shows how the path of trying to fulfill rival desires leads right to the final end of death. However, what this passage clearly points out is how these desires originate in a world system which is governed or dictated by a demonic influence and this system appears to be normal to those who live in it. It is a system which produces haughtiness, pride, arrogance or self-importance in those who are operating in the pursuit of its lusts. Yet it is those who are humble, modest, unassuming, and down-to-earth who receive grace from the Father to resist and overcome these assaults. Paul declares this in Titus.

Titus 2:11-12 KJVR

*(11) For the grace of God that brings salvation has
appeared to all men,*

*(12) Teaching us that, denying ungodliness and worldly
lusts, we should live soberly, righteously, and godly, in this
present world;*

I want to make a point here that both of these passages
show. Jesus, who Paul claims to the be the grace of God, is our
example of how to live this life yet it is our efforts to resist rival
desires which make this possible. Many, regrettably, believe
they can remain baby believers and have things spoon fed to
them, occasionally throwing a tantrum when their spiritual
diaper needs changed expecting Father to swoop in, gently pat
them on their bare bottom, offer cooing words of affirmation
and tidy up the mess.

Look, what happened in your pants is your doing because of
the diet you fed yourself. These passages clearly state we are
the one who is to resist the influences coming from others. As
you stay humble, according to James, Father gives you the grace,
or what may be better known as strength, to stand your ground
that will, through the process, finally cause you to be recognized
as a conqueror.

The reflection process...

Alright, let me, as a review, go over the particulars of this
mimesis process so you can make sure that you understand it on
a personal basis before I take you into the nature of it in a crowd

environment.   Everyone has desires, nothing wrong with that. We have to ask ourselves though, "Is this desire truly mine, did it originate from me, or am I mirroring a desire from another who is either around me now or from my past?"   The reason for this is to determine whether you are the model of this desire or the reflection from another model.

Now this step is fairly easy by yourself.   Call it personal reflection (pun intended), if you want.   Give yourself a look into what is motivating you to do something or act in a particular manner.   However, this is not going to work very well when you're in the space of another person.   The moment two mirror agents come in contact the reflection process begins.   Before you go and get all spook-weird on me, understand this has always been going on in your life and you've made it this far. Now you finally have the perception to recognize mimesis as it develops.   Yes, it may seem awkward at first as you adjust to this new field of vision but you'll soon settle in and be able to navigate just as you always have, just smarter.

Okay, let's say you are the model for a desire.   This desire has emotions, at least two, possible more, that drive it: The emotion which starts the desire and the emotion that makes you feel satisfied when it is completed.   If it takes an extended period of time to fulfill the desire, there is an emotion which will maintain the buoyant nature from the initial emotion, kind of like helium in a balloon you have to replace to keep it aloft. These might be considered the "nice" emotions of a desire. Regrettably, there is a dark side to emotions which I'll explain in a moment, so hang in there.   The point I clearly want to establish is that desires have emotions attached to them.   When an emotion manifests, don't get all hyper; determine what desire it is trying to lay bare.

So here is a simple example: Fred has the desire to go to the park and enjoy the sunny day. (He is the model.) He really wants to do this because it relaxes him. (This is the emotion driving the desire.) Fran comes into the room where Fred is and he asks her to go to the park with him. (She is a mirror agent.) The reflection process now begins.

At this point the interaction can go in two directions. Here is the first scenario. Fred has modeled his desire. The mirror agent receives the desire and reflects it back. From this point forward the mimetic cycle is like a poker game, I see your reflection and raise you my reflection. Fran responds that going to the park sounds great; why not make it a picnic? Fred thinks about how this will fit in with his desire and decides a picnic would work. Then he recalls a park that has a pond with canoes and this might be a fun thing to do. Fran thinks canoes might be a little much but Fred seems able to handle it, so she agrees and goes to prepare a basket. (At this point, Fran has "called" the desire wager and all the players are in.) Fred is happy to get out of the house. (Closing emotion for the desire has set in.)

Notice in this example how the desire is expressed to one and it is returned with an increased intensity which in turn is reflected back at a higher level also. This is common in the mimetic cycle where the reflected desire never comes back at the same level it was released. This is vital to understand in the interactions you have with others. I'm sure you have encountered situations where things seemed "to get out of hand" and never realized just how that could have happened. Now you know why. Remember mirrors reflecting mirrors reflecting mirrors reflecting...get the point?

I'm sure you've been waiting anxiously to find out what the other path our couple here could take with this mimetic cycle. In showing this I'll bring into play the "bad" emotions attached to a desire. Fred expresses his desire to go the park because it relaxes him. Fran looks at him and says she will if before they go he can fix the screen door which is loose and keeps falling off of its track. Fred, knowing how doing this would require him to dismantle a large portion of the door and time it takes finding all the tools and parts required to make this fix happen becomes frustrated by this delay. (This is a "bad" emotion indicating the desire is being hindered.) Fred reflects his frustration as a delay back to Fran by responding how he wants to handle it after they return. Fran becomes increasingly frustrated with Fred's planned delay and expresses back to him that he always keeps putting other things ahead of her desires which shows her that he doesn't really care about her. (The emotion of security is attached to her desire.) Fred takes this and becomes infuriated by how Fran would think he doesn't care about her and...well we all know how this is going to turn out, right? Fred may very well end up at the park, but not for reasons he originally intended.

There is a line from the movie *Cool Hand Luke* that fits this situation, "What we have here is a failure to communicate." In the mimetic cycle what is really happening is that there is a rival desire operating. The screen door in this instance is the scandal which accelerates the rival desire to a point where something will have to break. When rival desires collide the final solution is the elimination of one of the models of desire. However, that is overly simplistic. The dynamics involved in reaching the final solution on the other hand are as varied as the models involved and the emotions that are associated to the desires. What will occur as this cycle escalates is that desires, which had been the driver at the start of the cycle, will suddenly stop being the reflection. The emotions attached to the desire which were there to carry the desire out suddenly become the driver *and* the reflection given. Now this becomes a contest of betting on whose emotion can reach the highest point.

Once emotions have kicked in, the pressure in this matter will continue to build, it seems almost exponentially, until it comes to an impasse. If you're familiar with how a pressure cooker works, there is a device on it called a pressure relief valve which allows all the trapped steam to escape without causing the pot to explode. In the escalation of a mimetic cycle the same point of intense pressure will arise and something has to let the "steam" off for things to return to normal.

Often, an innocent victim is the final solution. A third party enters the scenario and becomes the relief valve to release the pent up emotions in the cycle. This victim, not knowing what is about to happen to them, may become the target of verbal or physical abuse; may be confronted for an insignificant behavior which now appears as a large obstacle; may be raked over the coals for a physical abnormality that inflames fear in the attacker; or may just have to endure the tirade of bad luck and hardship the assailant has had to endure from the other party in the mimetic cycle.

This pressure is not one-sided by any stretch of the imagination. It took two to build it and it will often require two victims to release it properly. Once the pressure has been relieved a sense of peace will return to the environment for a period of time and then the cycle will begin all over again.

The desires of many...

There are times when the emotions that are tied to the cycle have warped any sense of reality completely out of the picture on the part of both agents. The intention of the final solution is to eliminate the other agent. This brings us the victim, who may become part of an adulterous affair with one of the agents. I'm not going into the rightness or wrongness of this type of solution but I want to focus on the intention. It simply is to eliminate the other mimetic agent and the unbearable pressure that has been created. If you find this explanation too difficult to accept, then let me show you someone in the life of Jesus who was caught up in just this type of mimetic cycle but on a grander scale involving a mob.

In the eighth chapter of the book of John, Jesus has come to the temple to teach the people. The scribes and Pharisees who work there on the other hand have a different desire. They plan on trapping Jesus - yes they are preparing a scandal. What is the trap stick in this matter? The Law of Moses. Those 613 commandments they were experts at deciphering. The bait in this grand charade is none other than a woman, an adulterous woman, caught in the very act nonetheless! Have you ever stopped and wondered how these pious men of the temple elite knew where to find a woman in the very act of adultery? I mean, it's an act you don't readily broadcast for all to know about, particularly a priest. It's something you hide; primarily conducted in the dark recesses of backrooms or in locations away far from a spouse. Yet somehow these guys, who don't like being anywhere near sin, pluck this peach of a woman, and yet completely forget to also bring her accomplice, someone who apparently knew how to punch her dance card without letting anyone else tango with her.

The self-righteous cast the shame-filled woman towards Jesus and declare how the Law of Moses states that she should be stoned. What did Jesus think should be done they press? John tells us they make this claim in order to accuse Jesus. Interesting how they want to accuse him for their misdeeds. Anyway, things are heating up with these guys. They are trying to get Jesus to respond to their claims and he's not playing their game. Yes, it is a game of reflection poker on a grand scale. Each one of these stiff-collared men of the cloth is fuming. Why? They're mirroring each other. This is how a mob scene works. It's called a mimetic contagion. All these guys are putting into the pot expecting Jesus to play along not knowing he holds a royal flush and he is about to lay it down.

But wait; what is he doing? He is stooped down, writing in the sand with his finger! Not a stick, his finger, in the sand no less, and stooped down too! What is he thinking here? Doesn't he know these nitwits are out for blood? Is he ducking down to get out of the way of the debris field which is about to rain down about him? Do you know how hard it is to have an argument with someone who will not even look at you, let alone is

Stumbling Towards the Desire of Grace

preoccupied? And what on the earth is he writing? (Yes, I did say that. It was there and I just couldn't pass it up!) He better not be making hearts in the sand like some Joanie-loves-Chachie shtick. The last time we have any record of a deity-type using his finger to write is that ten commandment incident which these dudes seem so hotly invested in. So what is Jesus doing in the mimetic cycle before him?

Jesus is the model. He models the Father's desire. There is a saying that the eyes are the windows to the soul. Have you ever tried to write without looking at what you're writing? Dang near impossible to keep it legible at the least. But saying this would make you think that what Jesus wrote was important since this is the only record of him writing. IF these law-abiding religious types are incensed by mirroring the desires of each other, what do you think would happen to the woman the moment the gaze of Jesus met theirs? Come on, these guys came loaded for bear. Jesus was in their sights all along. He wasn't playing their game, a game being conducted at the temple in front of a crowd of people, who while not participating, were still reflecting the desires of these ignoble men. If his gaze connected with them even for a moment, their reflection would be displayed and amped up back at them. Then the girl is road pavement!

John tells us that as they continued to ask him what his thoughts were on the matter, Jesus finally arose and declares, "He who is without sin among you, let him cast the first stone." Sensing the point where the pressure is about to burst, Jesus rises and speaks. Doesn't he always rise and speak to you when the pressure is the greatest? Placed in a similar situation most people would immediately identify with these temple men. Sinless is not something they can claim about themselves. Sure, they appear to be sinless to the public, but there are those little personal sins which compromise their integrity when they are forced to judge themselves before others. So they began to disperse, the oldest to the youngest.

What if I told you there was something else at play here that aligns with the mimetic nature of these events, would you continue to read? Of course you would! Let's consider how the Law of Moses is correct. Anyone who is caught in the act of adultery must be stoned. This command is found in Leviticus 20:10 and Deuteronomy 22:22 and in each of these passages it clearly states that BOTH are to be stoned. So if you're going to inflict this punishment on one, the other gets it too. Yet there is something more in this judgment we miss today. There was a law which stated when a stoning was to take place it required two people to cast stones at the guilty first. Seriously consider this for a moment. Could you cast the first stone at someone convicted? To be the first is the model all others will follow. The most difficult thing for someone to do is be the model for an action that requires others to follow. You see, in order to carry out this punishment there not only has be a model, but there also has to be a mirror agent who will activate the other agents assigned with the task of carrying out the ruling.

So here is Jesus demanding this incensed, self-righteous mob to produce a model who has no sin, who is not an offense, who has not offended God, to cast the rock of offense. Then what does he do? Back to writing in the dust! Dude, I'm going to play this mimetic cycle for all it is worth. I don't even want you to look at me as you come down off of your emotionally-fed temper tantrum. Deal with the mess you've created in your own psyche. I'm going to play in the sand until you've come to your senses. The one thing I often wonder at this point is if he was writing in the sand, "Are they gone yet?" to his disciples.

Now comes the fun part to this message. Jesus is left with this woman and no one else. So he stands, looks at the woman and asks where her accusers are? Is there no one to accuse her? She has been brought from a deed that is unspeakable, so dark it is listed in the Ten Commandments! Thrust into public view as all scandals do, she no longer has the privilege of being hidden from the pointing finger and hidden innuendos. Those who saw her that day will forever carry her in their memory as a woman sullied at the hands of..."Neither do I..."

Remember what I stated, the bible is a story of victims. She was to be sacrificed to fulfill the desire of the Scribes and Pharisees. It mattered little about what caused her to be selected, and I can only guess that one of those who was a late comer to the mob had grown weary of her and decided how in order to reset his life, the only solution was to exact the final solution. So any way you want to look at this, she is a victim from one mimetic cycle between two people in conflict to another conflict which was designed to eliminate Jesus from influencing the public.

"Neither do I..."is the model she was searching for. It did not reflect what she felt about herself but what the Father saw in her. Despite what we may feel about ourselves, what we've done or not done, those things that cause us to hide from the

Father are really just illusions constructed to satisfy a sense of who we think God desires us to be. Let me put this as simply as I can: We don't have a clue. Dumb and dumber describes our nature and is the rightful title to the movie of our life.

"...offend no more." Sure, actually the text says "sin" but let me call you back to the beginning of this study where I stated how you needed to hold to this meaning of offend or offense, rather than what we've been indoctrinated with. How much of whom we are offends people? This is a sin, an offense. Our actions will always place people at a point of offense if they determine our actions to be something they cannot accept. This does not make us an offense; it only establishes their desires as being at odds to us. As far as God is concerned, all offenses have been dealt with in Jesus.

If there was one place I could place myself in the biblical narrative it would be as this woman. Think about the desire that is emanating from Jesus at this moment. He is seeing the desire of the Father for her at this moment and is reflecting it to her at a level increased higher than how he received it. The Father loves her beyond anything she has ever experienced in her life and she is being washed in this deeply, right to the core of who she is. Having just experienced the reprieve of formal justice she is now confronted with the model of a desire which she had sought in an affair yet never experienced: Love. Unlike the mob before her, she is given the privileged access to the reflection of Jesus, in whom the Father is well pleased, one who would change her entire world.

Stumbling Towards the Desire of Grace

In the book of John, Jesus claimed he only did those things that he saw his Father do. This mimetic claim is where we all now reside in Him. As Jesus looks into the face of the Father we reflect the love that is being displayed between them. The actions of our day in Him are the intentions of their love towards us. All we need do to address the rival desires which confront us is follow the pattern of the one in whom we are. Because as he is so are we in this world. But it's not as easy as it sounds, right?

The newness of old desires...

If you're looking for a high-octane New Testament book on the battle of rival desires then there is none better than the book of Galatians. It's a war from the get go! It is also the one book that clearly and forcibly defines the difference between the old and new covenant natures and types. Paul, chosen of God to be the apostle of the message of the kingdom of Grace, wastes no time in hitting the churches of Galatia up side their head with his claim how they have become so dull in thinking there is another message of grace other than what he preached to them. It seems some uppity members of the Jerusalem Jews troop came into the territory and claimed how what Paul was saying needed to include observing the customs of the Jews, including whacking off the tender part of a male's hinder parts!

Think about the seriousness of this for moment. Who in their right mind, or any mind for that matter, goes to a tent meeting and gets all jacked up in the excitement of God showing off, goes home and proclaims the greatness of God to his friends for days and weeks on end, only to come back to another meeting, where some expert-from-afar claims how your days of communing with your lovely will have to be curtailed while you heal? "Yup, that's me. He's gotta be telling the truth, look at him, all...all...get me my knife before your supple body changes my mind!"

Come on, people, don't you now see what is going on here? Rival desires have broken out and the crowd is mirroring the desire of an old nature found in these Jewish pulpiteers. Paul sees right through their conniving and launches the best combative verse in all the bible, "I wish they would cut off that which troubles you."

Throughout this book Paul gives his credentials for his message and then offers numerous examples from the history of Israel to demonstrate the superiority of the new covenant, which these Galatians were a part of, and the old covenant, limited to the children of Israel. It is at the end of the fifth chapter where Paul fully unveils the nature of the conflict these people are encountering. It all comes down to a lust, a desire, either by their flesh or by the Spirit who resides in them.

Galatians 5:13-15 KJVR

(13) For, brethren, ye have been called unto liberty; only use not liberty for an occasion to the flesh, but by love serve one another.

(14) For all the law is fulfilled in one word, even in this; Thou shalt love thy neighbor as thyself.

(15) But if ye bite and devour one another, take heed that ye be not consumed one of another.

Stumbling Towards the Desire of Grace

Notice what is happening in these few verses. Paul clearly lets them know they have been called into liberty, or freedom, with its intent to love and serve one another. Do you see the intention of freedom, the desire of liberty is to love and serve someone other than ourselves? Paul then states how The Law is fulfilled in the commandment that you should love your neighbor as yourself. This is all great and rosy but dang near impossible without the Spirit! Why? The last verse clearly states how the nature of the flesh operates: biting and devouring. Look familiar?

Rival desires cause us to bite and devour each other as we move towards the final solution of eliminating the rival. There is no love here, spiritual or otherwise. Two combatants slugging it out in the worst kind of urban warfare imagined. Sure, I'll love you, if you love me first, jerk! The mimetic cycle here has no chance of being diverted unless the Spirit gets involved. And the Spirit wants desperately to get involved but lusts, desires, and their emotions are raging like a 15-year-old male at the swimsuit portion of a Texas beauty pageant! Look at what the Spirit is up against.

Galatians 5:19-21 Mirror Translation

(19) The influence of the flesh is obvious: wherever a legalistic judgmental attitude prevails, sexual sins are rampant! Anything goes: adultery, filth ,and outrageous licentiousness;

(20) such as idolatry, which is worshipping a distorted image of oneself, drugs, hatred, constant conflict, jealous suspicion, violent outbursts of rage, everyone for himself in a cut-throat competitive world, trampling on others to

get to the top, dissension, heresy, and manipulating
people's mind with false teaching.

(21) Consumed with envious self pity, murder, drunken
stupor, intoxicating licentiousness and lust, with all the
quarrels and jealousy it ignites. As I have stated before:
those who are practicing this kind of lifestyle have
nothing in common with the Kingdom of God.

What was the reference I made earlier? Oh yeah, Black Friday in Las Vegas. Now I know there are those few out there who are cheering on the champion of our cause, Jesus, praying for him to step in and clock those miserable, senseless fools with a swift right cross to the jaw. If he does that, he'll knock all of us out! This is an area where we must do the work along side of the Spirit. We have to rely on Holy Spirit to convict us where rivalry manifests in our lives. The desires we have in these matters must be offered over to the Godhead for us to, first off, determine if they truly are ours. Then, and only then, can we dispose of them if they're not ours. If they are wise desires we then partner with Holy Spirit to see them fulfilled in the midst of a world caught up in achieving the final solution.

This is one of the paradoxes of the kingdom: We died in Christ, so our body is not our own. Yet we are asked to die daily to our will and desires. All the Father wants from you is for you to give up all your desires so He can give His desires to you. I know, it doesn't seem like a fair trade. It isn't – He loses every time you chose yours desires over His. But the Father, Jesus and Holy Spirit knew the risk going into this matter. A free agent with Their own will is all They're looking for. They know that "free will" also means the will to choose as one desires. Yet how many times have you cried out Him, "God, what is your will for my life? I only want to do your will!" You could just as easily be crying, "God, what is your desire for my life? I only want to do your desire!"

The World of...

1 John 2:16-17 KJVR

(16) For all that is in the world, the lust of the flesh, and the lust of the eyes, and the pride of life, is not of the Father, but is of the world.
(17) And the world passes away, and the lust thereof: but he that doeth the will of God abides forever.

I'm going to take a small turn in this discussion more akin to a bypass on a freeway that takes us around another area of town delivering us in the end to the same destination as the main road. This passage out of 1 John talks about the lust of the world. I trust you can see by now this term is a rich example of mirroring desires that are ramping to their extreme end. John is letting us know these episodes are worldly and will pass away with each new...whatever it is. Notice how he connects the mirroring of the will or desire of the Father with abiding forever.

What I want to draw your attention to in this passage is the claim John makes about the "pride of life." This pride of life issue is the claim and badge of honor that shows you've gotten everything you've every desired. It is a "works-based" principle that does not allow anyone or anything to share in your achievements. I wanted it; I planned for it; I fought long and hard for it, so keep your hands off! Examine this for moment.

James 4:5-7 KJVR

(5) Do ye think that the scripture says in vain, The spirit that dwells in us lusts to envy?
(6) But he gives more grace. Wherefore he said, God resists the proud, but gives grace unto the humble.
(7) Submit yourselves therefore to God. Resist the devil, and he will flee from you.

Verse 5 informs us that the Spirit is jealous for us. You read that right. Holy Spirit is a jealous lover who wants to give us desires we can't even begin to fathom. As you move into verse 6 you see how this gift is more grace. Show of hands, who doesn't want more grace? Now notice the next claim about who gets this increase of grace. I need to step in here and adjust the lens of your understanding.

The last part of verse 6 is actually a statement made from Proverbs 3:34. It sounds great and plays real well at grandma's apron strings but this is New Testament theology. So I'm about to twist your brain with this line of thinking.

John has declared how God is love and how he so loved the world that he gave his only Son, who according the writings of Paul is recognized as the embodiment of grace. Are you following me? God, as love, gave grace, his son, to the world. Peter tells us God is no respecter of persons, so this means there is not one single person who God did not give grace to, correct? Of course. So with this understanding of the generous, loving nature of our Father, is James accurately portraying the giving nature of the Father and Spirit from verse 5 if he is holding back on someone in verse 6?

Stumbling Towards the Desire of Grace

Permit me for a moment to offer a more truthful translation of verse 6.

James 4:6 Mike translation

(6) But he gives more grace. Despite what's been said before, God gives grace to all those who are humble but the gift is resisted by the proud.

Proud people don't want anything from anyone. It's by their hands and theirs alone. The Father wants to give and pour out in abundance to them, but they have shut off His ability to do so. God never resists them unless you want to step into the mimetic cycle of this and realize how James may be speaking of a mirroring event being transacted here from earth to heaven first!

If you've ever dealt with bratty children, there comes a point in your time with them when they will not listen to you or do what they need to do. Sure, you can exert your dominion and pull a power play on them, but this often doesn't work out for everyone. Sometimes, especially if you're at tirade level, the best thing is to let them just do their thing and see to it they don't bring any harm to themselves or others. This often gives them time to cool down where you can then take them aside and blister their...excuse me, redirect their attitude.

These kids are just being prideful. They want nothing to do with you; they're on the adventure of self awareness. You don't resist them as much as allow them to resist what you want to (truly) give them, if you catch my drift. At no point did you stop loving them and seeking their good. And despite this blip of emotional hysteria you still give to them as the day moves along. Now as Jesus said, if you, being bad people know how to give good things to your children, how much more will your Father in heaven give good things to you?

Consider claims like, "I don't need you," or, "God has never done anything for me," or "How come you always do this to me, God?" Is there a little pride poking out in these subtle stabs at a natural, other-loving giver? There is also out of James those verses, "You have not because you ask not... you receive not because you ask amiss to satisfy your desires." Prideful people are like that.

Let's also take note of these little stabs at Love's gift. How often have you been offended by God doing something in your life that went counter to how you thought it should turn out? You get so bent out of shape that you huff and fume around everyone telling them you're not going trust Him in this area again. Come on, fess up. I've done it, so I know you've done it at least once.

Recall that offense is merely a rival desire presented in a mimetic cycle. You were right there in the thick of it with the Father, Him expressing His desire to you, and suddenly you throw up this off-the-wall desire you're so certain is the best thing for your life. You sense God say no and then it's off to the races with your silly self, chucking every good thing God intends for you out the window so you can ski in Sweden with the blue-eyed-blond-hair-Adonis Claus when you've never skied in your life. And if you think I'm being a little one-sided in this cycle how about you Evinrude/Harley Davison crowd who will exploit an opportunity to experience the quiet frontier rather than...you know what I mean.

Often in these instances we are so enamored by the thought of obtaining the affection of our desire, which despite all the warnings, bells, alarms and just plain NO! that confronts us, we're going to plow, push or plunge ahead of everyone around us. Be assured, not for one moment do we believe, let alone even think we're being prideful, but...

All the Father is asking you to do is turn to Holy Spirit so that you can begin reflecting the desire Jesus has for you in the presence of the Father. It is an act you are solely in charge of doing if you want to truly be in the image and likeness of Him.

I leave you with the following which comes from C.S. Lewis' *The Weight of Glory* and speaks volumes to the desire the Father has for us compared to ours.

> *Indeed, if we consider the unblushing promises of reward and the staggering nature of the rewards promised in the Gospels, it would seem that Our Lord finds our desires not too strong, but too weak. We are half-hearted creatures, fooling about with drink and sex and ambition when infinite joy is offered us, like an ignorant child who wants to go on making mud pies in a slum because he cannot imagine what is meant by the offer of a holiday at the sea.*

CLOSING THOUGHTS

How do I...

This is a common response from anyone who reads this material. They want to implement it into their life with some set of guidelines or planned out routine. I can't offer that to you. Why? Do you really want to mirror me? The Father is who you're to direct yourself towards and this is accomplished by looking to Jesus. Holy Spirit will show you how to do...just ask. It is something that you're entirely responsible for; meaning you have to initiate it and follow through.

Jealous of this?

When was the last time you were jealous because your neighbor watched television or mowed his yard? Or how about the last time your coworker drove to work? Or perhaps the last time your spouse washed clothes?

All of those things are pretty ridiculous reasons to be jealous I'll admit. Being jealous means you see something that someone else has and you feel the desire to have the same thing. It's not a small desire but a burning passion that can cause you to even become highly enraged in certain instances. Take a moment to remember a moment you were jealous of someone and what it was you so adamantly desired to have. Feel the passion once again rise within you at just the mere thought of this. Jealousy is pretty powerful.

The Apostle Paul writes in chapters 9 thru 11 of the book of Romans about his earnest desire to see his family members of the household of Israel to see the truth of what God has done through Jesus Christ. He recounts many passages from the prophets and the law which clearly indicate how Israel's unbelief and adherence to the works of the law has blinded them to the grace of God. As you come to the close of the eleventh chapter Paul makes a remarkable claim. His desire is that Israel will become so jealous of the grace shown to the Gentiles they will finally have their eyes open and embrace the gospel of grace which he is a minister of.

This is a remarkable statement that cannot be seen, let alone claimed to be in action anywhere in the church today. How can I make such a claim? Look at your church, or even yourself as a believer. What would make Israel jealous? What do you have they intensely desire to possess? Practically every church looks and operates just like the Jews do in the following of The Law. Yet Paul says it is The Law that has blinded Israel to the message of grace. Well if Israel is blinded by it, how can the church not experience its same effect?

Paul is quite clear it is the message of grace, the new covenant, the new creation realities found in the finished works of Christ that are the driving factors to what will make Israel jealous. I know this is hard to accept, but as long as your life and the community of believers you associate with are bound to anything from The Law you aren't that special. You're just plain. There is nothing super about you that anyone will be jealous about. In other words, you lack the ability to change the hearts and minds of people. In the spirit of this message you just read, there is nothing people want to mirror as a desire from you. In other words, you're desire-less. Only grace will make you desirable.

Now there's something most preachers won't even think about telling you grace is capable of doing. Why? Because the moment they begin preaching the truth about the liberty found in grace they know they will lose control of the people they have gathered around them. Kind of a oxymoron approach isn't it? You want people to experience the freedom found in Christ but not the freedom from you controlling them? The true, unfiltered, pure word of God's grace cuts through all that **** and will make people who don't have it, jealous...period. So why not make it your mission to just make people jealous of you? I dare you!

About the Author

Mike and his family live in Portland, Oregon, where he is one of the teachers of the Word of God at a local fellowship in Clackamas, Oregon. As a graduate of the Latin University of Theology, Mike is passionate about people understanding what the Kingdom of God is, its impact in their lives and how it changes communities that are determined to operate from its authority.

Mike is the author of *Grace for Shame*, *Chesed: Beyond the Veil of Mercy* and *Your Life is a Freaking Mess and You Want Answers*, and *A Kingdom Primer – The Basics to the Kingdom of God*. Mike also contributes his insights about the kingdom of grace at www.graceforshame.com and www.mygrace2u.com.

Chesed
Beyond the Veil of Mercy

mike hillebrecht

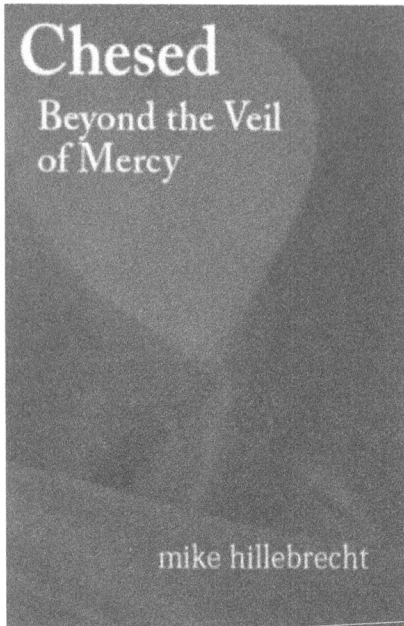

Additional titles by mike hillebrecht

What if what you knew from scriptures about mercy wasn't quite accurate? What if the blessings that we've been searching for have been locked away all this time in a simple Hebrew word that scholars agree has no English translation?

In this brief expose, teacher and author Mike Hillebrecht (Grace for Shame) explores the meaning of a Hebrew term that the original Bible scholars may have interpreted inaccurately into the Greek word we know as 'mercy. "You will begin to see how many of the Old and New Testament passages take on an entirely different meaning by understanding this key Hebrew word in its proper context.

Mike will take you through a practical explanation of the full meaning of coming to the throne of grace in God's Kingdom not with the expectation of judgment but with the fullest measure of equality. This is an eye-opening study that will impact your walk with the Lord and those that are around you.

Chesed – Beyond the Veil of Mercy
ISBN/EAN13:0615617352 / 9780615617350
Page Count: 70
Related Categories: Religion / Biblical Studies / General

www.beyondthemercyveil.com

Shame. Embarrassment. Humiliation. The ugly trio. Their distinct occupation is to keep you seeing yourself as a sinner saved by grace rather than as a son seated next to the throne of grace. The distinction is about whether you are being reigned over or whether you're reigning. It's a battle for your predestined role in the Kingdom of God.

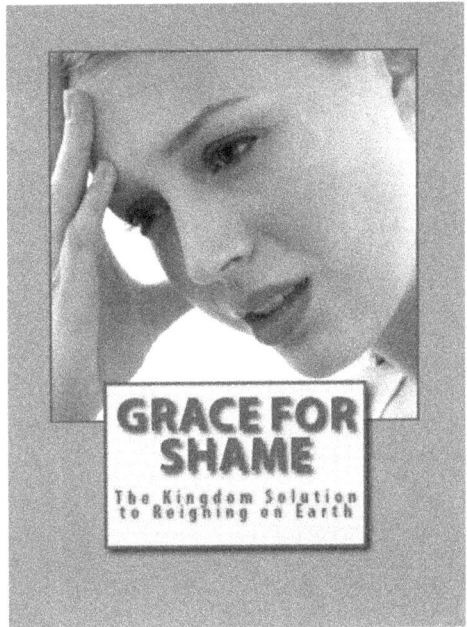

Inside *Grace for Shame* you will discover a fresh look at what grace truly looks like and how God designed it to operate in your life. This ain't your papa or mama's grace - this is grace straight from the Kingdom of God as it has been operating throughout all of eternity. You will find the grace that is intended to break off the shackles that the ugly trio has bound you with, imprisoning you from your destiny.

Expect to finally identify with the true kingdom meaning of the cross - not the sanitized message that religion has produced. Are you considered a prodigal son, or know someone who is? *Grace for Shame* gives a perspective from the Kingdom of God that it's not about your past but about how truly great you are right now in the eyes of the Father.

Grace for Shame
ISBN/EAN13: 0615605508 / 9780615605500
Page Count: 220
Related Categories: Religion / Christian Life / Personal Growth

www.graceforshame.com

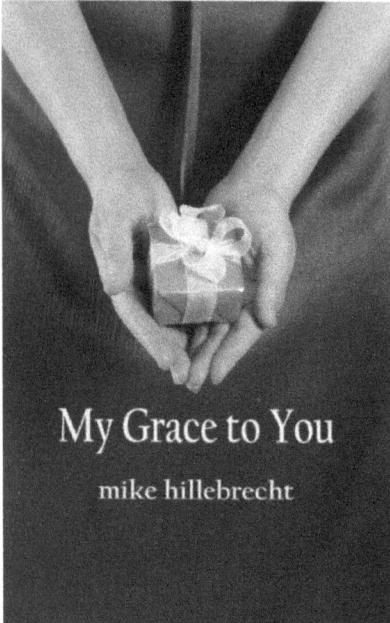

Most people study grace from the position of the fall of man. This makes grace an escape mechanism to get you into Heaven. But what if that wasn't the original intent of grace for you?

In *My Grace to You*, author mike hillebrecht takes a fresh look at grace from the Kingdom of God viewpoint before the foundation of the world. In this insightful reading you will discover why understanding how the New Testament writers use of grace in their daily social structures gave them an ability to activate the truths and power of the Kingdom of God quickly within their communities.

Drawing from a variety of sources, mike takes you on a well rounded tour of the meaning of grace that will open up possibilities which you may never knew existed. You can be certain this isn't the grace your grandma knew – and it sure is a whole lot more exciting too!

My Grace to You

ISBN-13: 978-0615686622 (Custom)
ISBN-10: 0615686621
Page Count: 202 pages
Related Categories: Religion / Christian Life / Personal Growth

www.mygrace2u.com

If you desire to be known as a Son of God according to Romans 8, you had better know the 3-R's of the Kingdom. They are the foundational tenets of the kingdom's interaction with you as a son. The Holy Spirit will not advance you to the head of the class if you miss any one of the important lessons these have to demonstrate. Within this booklet you will find covered the following items:

The Father's intent — What was the original intent of God and how it changed.

Reconciliation — The Father's plan.

Redemption — The purpose of Jesus

Righteousness — The effect of reconciliation and redemption.

Right of Law — Where you are in God's time-line.

Royal Law — This is the one law given by the King.

Perfect Law — This is what we're striving to adhere too.

Peace — It may not be what you think.

As with the purpose of any primer, the entire spectrum of the topics offered cannot be presented to their fullest measure. This book is designed simply to be a building block which will provoke your thoughts about the matters at hand and spur you to search out further how they impact your walk with the Father.

A Kingdom Primer

ISBN/EAN13: 061562099X / 978-0615620992

Page Count: 126 pages

Related Categories: Religion / Biblical Studies / General

www.kingdomprimer.com

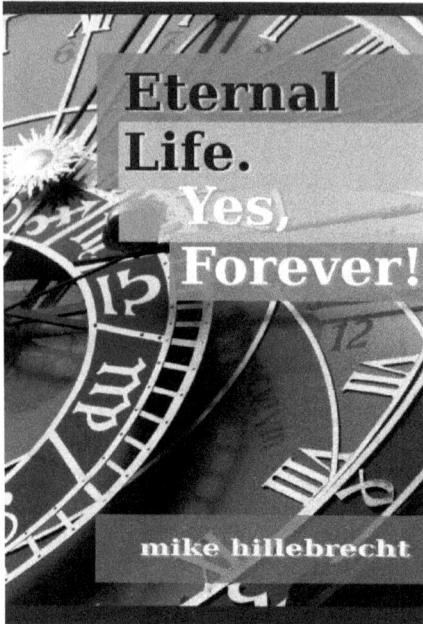

Live and not die! This is not the motto of some whacked out group of mercenaries. It belongs to a select group of people who believe that what Jesus Christ accomplished at the cross is supposed to be the norm for their lives.

What do you mean, "Thank goodness this isn't for me?"

Eternal life. Yes, Forever! is a stark look at a truth that has been turned sideways. Contained within, you will finally find the truth about the purpose of Heaven and how you're not supposed to go there except for dinner. Being "born again" versus being "saved" will be explored in relation to your dinner guests and football enthusiasts. You'll be re-introduced to the marvelous prefix "re" and see how this simple little construct, when it's added to a word, can screw up your entire theology.

Prepare to see death from an entirely different perspective as *Eternal Life. Yes, Forever!* takes off the gloves and slaps the enemy senseless once again.

Eternal Life. Yes, Forever!
ISBN-13: 978-0615623542 (Custom)
ISBN-10: 0615623549
Page Count: 140 pages
Related Categories Religion / Christian Life / Spiritual Growth

www.lifeyesforever.com

Do you perceive grace? This is a rather difficult question to answer for most people. The reason is they don't know or recognize what grace truly is. They've been taught a number of doctrinal positions on what it is but honestly, perceiving it, this is another matter. Perception is a matter of being able to discern, to determine or distinguish something which most often isn't readily visible or apparent. It's a hunch, a gut feeling, a premonition that conditions are leading to something...

There's Only Grace

Whether you perceive it or not

mike hillebrecht

The dilemma is you must actively search for conditions that warrant the existence of a perception to be noticed. This is work. This is why most people never question their perceptions about anything. They picked through the bits and pieces that were presented to them from some book (like this one), a speaker, a podcast, movie, song, or a drunken party of friends and adopt it as theirs never to consider the validity for it in their life. If the shoe fits, wear it.

Author and teacher mike hillebrecht is about to take you on a journey into how our thoughts and belief structures miss the very face of grace which is staring us right in the eye. Drawing from numerous personal revelations and biblical study, mike will "take a weed whacker to your thoughts an open a hole for truth to appear to you," so that you will be able to recognize grace operating in your life at all times.

There's Only Grace

ISBN-13: 978-0692363652
ISBN-10: 0692363653
Page Count: 140
Related Categories Religion / Christian Life / Spiritual Growth

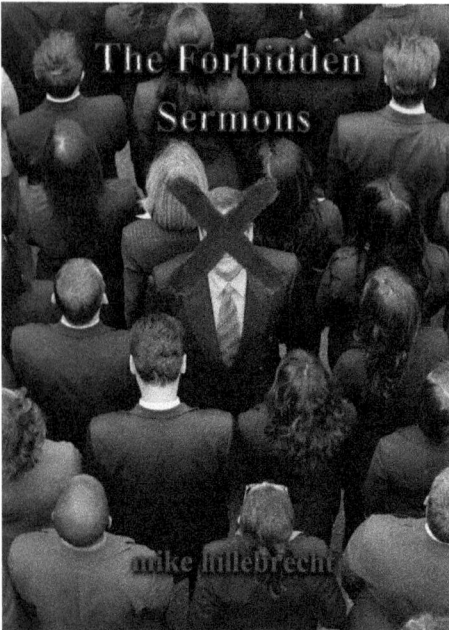

Tim has reached a critical juncture in his ministry: Get out or change. His wife Lisa wants out because she has had it with the people in this community of believers. Tim is leaning that direction too, there is someone who he once met that might have an answer for him on how to change things around.

Leon knows the difficulty of training a body of believers wrapped up in their sin consciousness towards what is the truth of their identity in Christ. Tim's story after all was his own many years prior. However, providence intervened for him and now it is his time to return the gesture with Tim.

Prepare to hear the message that the majority of pastors across the country aren't able to preach to their congregations. Hear the truth of the gospel of God's kingdom as it was preached in the first church. Learn how the identity of every person on this earth is being kept under wraps by a series of behavior modification programs being administrated not by the enemy, but rather by the church itself.

The Forbidden Sermons
ISBN-13: 978-0615985503
ISBN-10: 0615985505
Page Count: 166
Related Categories Religion / Christian Life / Spiritual Growth

did you like the book?

It has been my hope that contained within the contents of this book there has been one item, possibly more, which has inspired you or brought clarity to the path you're now following. If this is the case, then I would like to hear from you about what you discovered. You can write me at mike@mikehillebrecht.com.

Within the spirit of grace contained within this message, there is one of several other things you can now do. Books are promoted mostly by word of mouth. So if you found this useful, tell a friend. Heck, tell all your friends. Mention it on Facebook or whatever other social medium you use. If you're so inclined, you could go onto Amazon.com, look up the book and press the like button. While you're there, write a short review, or a long one if you like, about what you felt the book meant to you. If you're really inspired, give a copy to a pastor. However, considering the message, caution might be advised on this last one.

If none of these things interest you, I understand. Many of us don't feel it is right to compel others to view matters such as grace on the same plane as us. After all there are better things to have a dialogue about and not risk the chance of turning people off. But isn't this the reason that the risk was originally taken by Jesus – to turn people. So what have you got to lose? It's not you, but Christ who lives in you.

Thank you and my sincere gratitude.

Mike

Stumbling Towards the Desire of Grace

www.ingramcontent.com/pod-product-compliance
Lightning Source LLC
Chambersburg PA
CBHW071844020426
42331CB00007B/1848